3.8

W9-CFC-460

Tell Me Why

WHY?

I Cry

Katie Marsico

Published in the United States of America by Cherry Lake Publishing
Ann Arbor, Michigan
www.cherrylakepublishing.com

Content Adviser: Charisse Gencyuz, M.D., Clinical Instructor, Department of Internal Medicine,
University of Michigan
Reading Adviser: Marla Conn, ReadAbility, Inc.

Photo Credits: © bonzodog/Shutterstock Images, cover, 1, 21; © Samuel Borges Photography/Shutterstock Images,
cover, 1, 9; © rmnoa357/Shutterstock Images, cover, 1, 5; © RonGreer.Com/Shutterstock Images, cover, 1, 17;
© Julija Sapic/Shutterstock Images, cover, 1; © Lane V. Erickson/Shutterstock Images, cover, 1, 5; © michaeljung/
Shutterstock Images, back cover; © federicofoto/Shutterstock Images, 7; © Andrea Danti/Shutterstock Images, 9;
© Artmim/Shutterstock Images, 11; © Todd Castor/Shutterstock Images, 13; © Concept Photo/Shutterstock Images,
15; © Blend Images/Shutterstock Images, 19; © Zurijeta/Shutterstock Images, 21

Library of Congress Cataloging-in-Publication Data

Marsico, Katie, 1980- author.
 I cry / by Katie Marsico.
     pages cm. -- (Tell me why)
 Summary: "Offers answers to questions about those salty tears.
Explanations and appealing photos encourage readers to continue their quest
for knowledge. Text features, including a glossary and an index, help
students locate information and learn new words."-- Provided by publisher.
 Audience: K to grade 3.
 Includes bibliographical references and index.
 ISBN 978-1-63188-004-9 (hardcover) -- ISBN 978-1-63188-047-6 (pbk.) --
ISBN 978-1-63188-133-6 (ebook) -- ISBN 978-1-63188-090-2 (pdf) 1.
Tears--Juvenile literature--Miscellanea. 2. Eye--Juvenile
literature--Miscellanea. 3. Emotions--Juvenile literature--Miscellanea. 4.
Children's questions and answers. I. Title.

 QP231.M37 2015
 612.8'4--dc23
                        2014005662

Cherry Lake Publishing would like to acknowledge the work of The Partnership for 21st Century Skills. Please visit
www.p21.org for more information.

Printed in the United States of America
Corporate Graphics Inc.

Table of Contents

A Time for Tears

Today is the big day! Mia and her family are moving to a new town. It's almost time to go. Before they leave, Mia's friend Sam stops over to say good-bye.

Usually, Mia and Sam are always smiling and laughing when they are together. Yet today is different. As Mia hugs Sam, her eyes blur. Soon, tears drip past her eyelashes and onto her nose. Wait a minute…what's up with the waterworks?

Crying is a physical **reaction** to emotions, or feelings. A person's body

What if people weren't able to produce tears? Do you think they would be able to see as well?

Crying is a natural way to express many different emotions, including sadness.

responds to emotions such as sorrow by releasing tears. A tear is a drop of salty **fluid** that forms in the eye.

Tears are triggered by more than sadness. Basal tears are always present in people's eyes —even when they're happy! Their purpose is to provide **moisture**. Without basal tears, a person's eyes would dry out. Meanwhile, reflex tears are almost like a watery shield. They protect people's eyes from smoke, wind, dust, and other **irritants**.

Outdoor allergies sometimes cause tears.

Please Pass the Tissues!

Mia needs a tissue! Her cheeks are wet, and her nose is running. She feels like her whole face has turned into a faucet!

Tears are made up of three layers. They are oil, water, and a slimy substance called mucus. **Glands** along the edge of the eyelids create the oil. The water comes from glands beneath the eyebrows. Mucus is produced by **cells** on the outer surface of the eyes and along the inner eyelids.

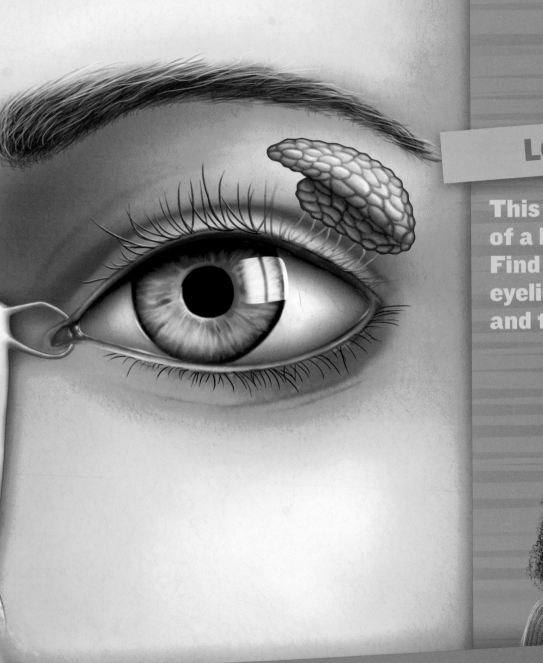

LOOK!

This is a picture of a human eye. Find the eyeball, eyelids, eyelashes, and tear duct.

Different parts of your eye work together to produce tears.

9

When people blink, their eyelids brush across their eyes. This motion sweeps tears into **ducts**, or drains, at the eyelids' inner corners. The ducts act as tiny passageways. They carry tears to the airways in a person's nose. Eventually, tears drain into the throat.

The result is that crying often causes a runny nose. It also produces a salty taste in the mouth.

People swallow their own tears when they cry.

From Feeling to Fluid

Mia didn't plan to cry. Still, she can't help but be upset about leaving Sam. Sorrow is an emotion. Mia isn't able to see or touch it. On the other hand, she feels and even tastes her tears! Mia wonders how her feelings turn into fluid that runs down her face.

Crying often involves both your body and inner feelings.

Crying is a process that begins in the brain. This **organ** controls how people think, move, and experience feelings. The brain responds to sadness by triggering the release of hormones.

Hormones are special chemicals made by the body. As they travel within the body, hormones help control how cells and organs do their work. These chemicals cause glands in and near the eye to produce tears.

When you think about something sad, hormones are released.

Scientists believe a certain amount of crying is good for people's health. They think being upset leads to a buildup of body chemicals. It's possible that crying helps flush out these waste products.

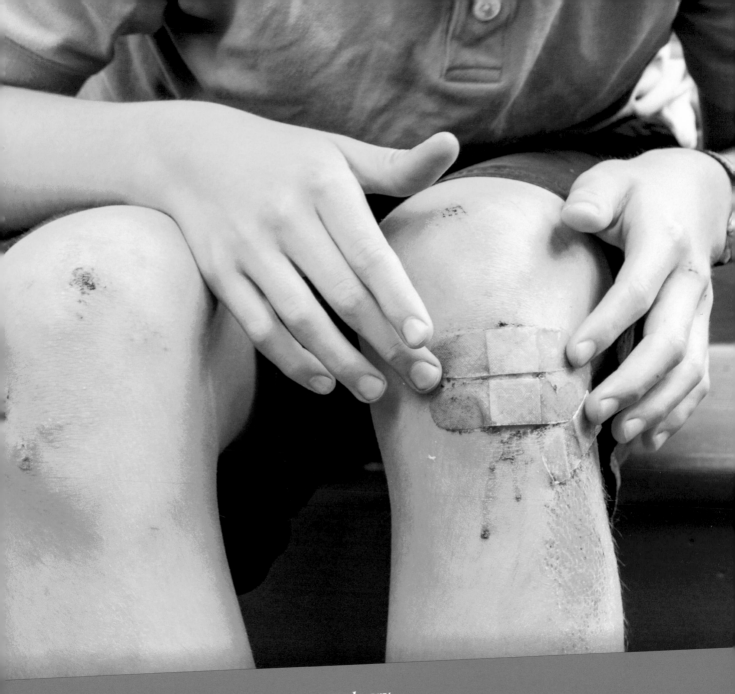

Physical pain sometimes makes people cry.

Cracking Up or Crying?

Mia looks down at Sam's shirt. It's all wet from Mia's teardrops. Sam jokes that Mia has her own built-in sprinkler system. Suddenly, the friends are giggling. In fact, they laugh so hard that they start to ... cry!

Tears are triggered by all kinds of **intense** emotions. Sorrow is one. Happiness is another.

Have you ever laughed so hard that you cried?

The brain often has the same reaction to different types of extreme feelings. It tells the body to release hormones. In turn, people's eyes form tears.

Today, Mia has shed tears of sadness *and* joy. Either way, she feels better after a good cry. When she hugs Sam for the last time, she has dry eyes and an ear-to-ear smile!

What else do you want to know about crying and tears? Write a list with at least three questions and head online—or to your local library!

Crying might actually help you feel better.

Think About It

Find a few photographs in magazines showing scenes that might cause eye irritation. What is going on that would trigger tears?

Do you think other animals besides humans cry? Go online with an adult or visit your library to find the answer.

Think about a play, a movie, or a television show where an actor was crying. How do you think actors are able to produce tears at just the right time?

Glossary

cells (SELZ) tiny units that are the building blocks of all living things

ducts (DUHKTZ) channels or passageways through which body substances travel

fluid (FLOO-uhd) a substance such as water that has no fixed shape and that flows easily

glands (GLANDZ) organs that produce substances used by the body

intense (in-TENTS) extreme or very strong

irritants (IR-uh-tuhntz) things that produce discomfort or pain

moisture (MOYS-chure) a small amount of liquid that makes something wet

organ (OR-guhn) a body part such as the brain that performs a specific job

reaction (ree-AK-shuhn) response

shed (SHED) to lose, get rid of, or let something fall

Find Out More

Books:

Enslow, Brian. *My Eyes*. Berkeley Heights, NJ: Enslow Publishers, 2011.

Landolfi, Libby. *What Happens When I Cry?* Milwaukee: Gareth Stevens Publishing, 2014.

Spelman, Cornelia Maude. *When I Feel Sad*. New York: AV2 by Weigl, 2013.

Web Sites:

KidsHealth—Why Do Eyes Water?
> *http://kidshealth.org/kid/talk/qa/eyes_water.html?tracking=K_RelatedArticle*
> Learn additional fun facts about tears and why people's eyes water.

ScienceWithMe!—Why Do Onions Make Us Cry?
> *http://sciencewithme.com/why-do-onions-make-us-cry*
> Check out a cool science experiment (to try with an adult) that will teach you more about tears.

Index

About the Author

Katie Marsico is the author of more than 150 children's books. She lives in a suburb of Chicago, Illinois, with her husband and children.